Armadillos
Dynamite Diggers

By Susan Knopf

Children's Press®
An Imprint of Scholastic Inc.

Content Consultant
Animal Programs Staff
Columbus Zoo and Aquarium

Library of Congress Cataloging-in-Publication Data
Names: Knopf, Susan, author.
Title: Armadillos: dynamite diggers/by Susan Knopf.
Description: New York, NY: Children's Press, an imprint of Scholastic Inc., 2020. | Series: Nature's children | Includes index.
Identifiers: LCCN 2019004829| ISBN 9780531229880 (library binding) | ISBN 9780531239100 (paperback)
Subjects: LCSH: Armadillos—Juvenile literature.
Classification: LCC QL737.E23 K56 2020 | DDC 599.3/12—dc23

Design by Anna Tunick Tabachnik

Creative Direction: Judith E. Christ for Scholastic Inc.

Produced by Spooky Cheetah Press

Printed in Heshan, China 62

SCHOLASTIC, CHILDREN'S PRESS, NATURE'S CHILDREN™, and associated logos
are trademarks and/or registered trademarks of Scholastic Inc.

1 2 3 4 5 6 7 8 9 10 R 29 28 27 26 25 24 23 22 21 20

Scholastic Inc., 557 Broadway, New York, NY 10012.

Photographs ©: cover: Rolf Nussbaumer/NPL/Minden Pictures; 1: lalito/Shutterstock; 4 top: Jim McMahon/Mapman®; 4 leaf silo
and throughout: stockgraphicdesigns.com; 5 child silo: Nowik Sylwia/Shutterstock; 5 armadillo sketch: mamita/Shutterstock;
5 bottom: Biosphoto/Superstock; 6 armadillo silo and throughout: Farhad Bek/Shutterstock; 7: Mark Payne-Gill/Nature Picture
Library/Getty Images; 8: Rosa Jay/Shutterstock; 10-11: Julia Christe/agefotostock; 12-13: Nicholas Smythe/Science Source;
15: Gabriel Rojo/NPL/Minden Pictures; 16-17: Claus Meyer/Minden Pictures/age fotostock; 19 top left: Victor Suarez Naranjo/
Shutterstock; 19 top right: Maryna Pleshkun/Shutterstock; 19 bottom left: James Davies/Alamy Images; 19 bottom right: Wanida_
Sri/Shutterstock; 20-21: Bianca Lavies/Getty Images; 22-23: Heidi and Hans-Juergen Koch/Minden Pictures; 25: Gunter
Ziesler/Getty Images; 26-27: Bianca Lavies/Getty Images; 28-29: Bianca Lavies/Getty Images; 30-31: belizar/Shutterstock;
33: Roman Garcia Mora/Stocktrek Images/Getty Images; 34-35: Damsea/Shutterstock; 37: Vera Storman/Getty Images;
38-39: Kevin Schafer/Getty Images; 40-41: Heidi and Hans-Juergen Koch/Minden Pictures; 42 left: Lucas Bustamante/Nature
Picture Library; 42 right: Eric Isselee/Shutterstock; 43 top left: Kevin Schafer/Getty Images; 43 top right: Joel Sartore/Getty
Images; 43 bottom left: Joel Sartore/Getty Images; 43 bottom right: Robert Eastman/Shutterstock; 48: Annie Watt.

◀ **Cover image
shows a nine-banded
armadillo sniffing for
something to eat!**

Table of Contents

Fact File: Armadillos

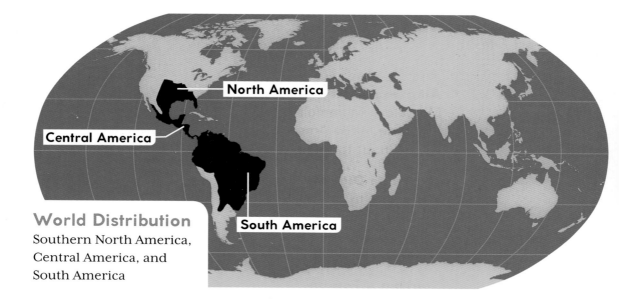

North America

Central America

South America

World Distribution
Southern North America, Central America, and South America

Habitat
Grasslands, savannas, rain forests, scrublands, and wetlands

Habits
Lives in underground burrows; sleeps up to 18 hours a day; can swim or walk along a river bottom

Diet
Insects, small animals, and vegetation

Distinctive Features
Body, face, and tail with a flexible shell-like covering; long nose, short legs, and long claws; poor eyesight, good sense of smell

Fast Fact
Armadillos are the only mammals with a shell-like covering.

Size Range

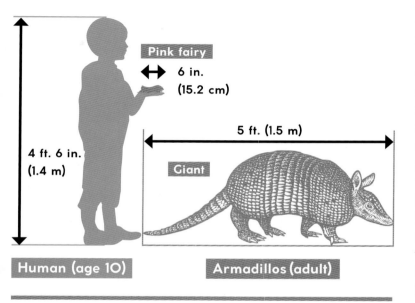

Pink fairy
↔ 6 in.
(15.2 cm)

5 ft. (1.5 m)

Giant

4 ft. 6 in.
(1.4 m)

Human (age 10)

Armadillos (adult)

Classification

CLASS
Mammalia
(mammals)

ORDER
Cingulata
(armadillos and five
extinct families of
animals)

FAMILY
Dasypodidae
(armadillos)

GENUS
Eight genera

SPECIES
20 species, including:
Tolypeutes tricinctus
(Brazilian three-
banded)
Chaetophractus vellerosus
(screaming hairy)
Priodontes maximus
(giant)

◀ **This screaming
hairy armadillo is
using its good sense of
smell to sniff out food.**

CHAPTER 1

Amazing Armadillos

A little armadillo rises on its back legs, peering above the tall grasses of its **savanna** home. It balances on its tail. Pointing its nose in the air, the armadillo turns its head from side to side. It can't see well, but it has a **keen** sense of smell.

The armadillo senses danger. A large animal is moving nearby. There's no time to run and no place to hide. The armadillo quickly folds its body into a ball. Then it tucks in its head, legs, and tail. A jaguar approaches and paws at the animal, which is fully encased in its armored shell. Eventually the frustrated **predator** wanders off.

This may be what comes to mind when you hear the word "armadillo." But did you know that only two of the 20 **species** of armadillos—the Brazilian three-banded and the southern three-banded—can do this?

▶ To untuck, armadillos take their heads and tails out first.

Hair
helps armadillos feel what's around them.

Hard Shell
is made of bony plates and provides protection.

Slender Snout
is good for sniffing out food.

Claws
are strong and curved for ripping up insect nests.

Strong Legs
give power for digging, running, and jumping.

Tail
can be round or flat and is covered with bony plates.

Marvelous Mammals

Armadillos are **mammals**, just as humans are. They come in different colors, including gray, brown, yellow, and pink. Many species have long **snouts**, while some have shorter ones. They have short, peg-shaped teeth and long tongues with sticky saliva. At the ends of their stout legs are strong, sharp claws. They all have a hard outer shell called a **carapace**.

Like cars, armadillos have hard tops and sides. Their underbellies are unprotected. Bands of bony plates called **scutes** cover their backs. These are made of bone and covered with keratin, the same material found in human hair and fingernails. The bands of armor alternate with stretchy skin, making armadillos flexible.

A protective shield covers the armadillo's face. In most species, the tail is covered with bony plates, too. Some armadillos are hairier than others, but they all have hair on their sides and bellies. This helps them sense the ground as they move around.

◄ A six-banded armadillo has up to eight bands.

Fast Fact
A turtle's shell is also called a carapace.

At Home in the Americas

Armadillos live in warm areas in South America, Central America, and southern North America. They can't live in cold places. Unlike most other mammals, armadillos have a slow **metabolism**. That means they have trouble regulating their body temperature. They don't store enough fat in their bodies to stay warm in cooler areas.

Armadillo **habitats** include rain forests, wetlands, scrublands, savannas, and grasslands. Some species need to live in a particular habitat, while others can thrive in different places.

The screaming hairy armadillo is found east of the Andes Mountains in South America, in the Monte Desert, where it is warm and dry. The giant armadillo lives throughout northern South America in many different habitats, including savanna, rain forest, and forest areas.

The nine-banded armadillo is the only species that lives in the United States. It is commonly found across the southern and southeastern region, from Texas to Florida. But it has been spotted as far north as Nebraska. It also lives in Central America.

▶ The weather in a hot, dry desert is just right for armadillos.

tail

snout

From Snout to Tail

Most armadillos are from 1 to 2 feet (0.3 to 0.6 meters) long, but there are some major exceptions. The pink fairy armadillo averages just 6 inches (15.2 centimeters) long and weighs only 6 ounces (0.2 kilograms). That's a little smaller than a hamster. The giant armadillo averages 5 ft. (1.5 m) long from head to tail and weighs 60 to 75 pounds (27.2 to 34 kg). That's about the size of a golden retriever. A nine-banded armadillo falls somewhere in between. It is about the size a house cat.

Some armadillos have long tails, and others have very short ones. The pink fairy armadillo has the shortest tail of all. It's only 1 in. (2.5 cm) long. That's not even as long as your thumb! The three-banded armadillo has a short tail, too. It's easy to tuck in when the armadillo rolls up into a ball. No surprise: the giant armadillo's tail is about 20 in. (50.8 cm). That's almost as long as three pencils!

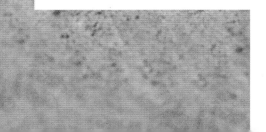

◀ The pink fairy armadillo is nocturnal and rarely seen during the day.

CHAPTER 2

Dynamite Diggers

All armadillo species have one thing in common—they are experts at digging! That's thanks to the long, curved claws on their front paws. As they dig, the animals push loose dirt away with their hind legs to keep the area clear. Armadillos dig quickly, holding their breath to keep dirt out of their mouths.

Digging is a very important survival skill for armadillos. They dig to create their homes, which are called **burrows**, and the tunnels inside the burrows. They also dig holes to hide in and to find food.

Armadillos choose places to live where the digging is easy. Some live in desertlike areas with sandy soil, which is loose and easy to dig through. Others prefer to live near rivers or streams, where the soil is damp and loose. For many, a tree is a favorite spot to dig. A burrow dug under tree roots means a sturdy roof overhead.

▶ This armadillo is digging a burrow where it can stay cool during the heat of the day.

Burrowing In

As a general rule, armadillos live alone. And each one may have up to a dozen active burrows at a time.

An armadillo burrow is large, up to 25 ft. (7.6 m) long. It may have several different living areas that are connected by tunnels. Each burrow has multiple entrances for quick entry and escape.

An armadillo marks the area around its burrow with urine and a strong odor produced by scent **glands** on its backside. These markings warn other animals to stay away.

Because armadillos are such fast diggers, building new burrows is easy work for them. It takes about 15 minutes to dig a new big burrow. So if food in an armadillo's home area becomes scarce, or if there's a **drought**, the animal will move to a new area and start over.

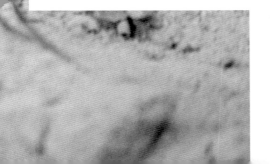

◀ A hungry armadillo leaves its burrow to hunt.

A Nose for Food

Armadillos are **omnivores**. Their diet is mostly insects, but armadillos also eat other animals, such as small lizards, spiders, and worms. They may also eat **carrion**, fruit, and plants. They use their short teeth to crunch through food they can't swallow whole.

Armadillos are **nocturnal**. They spend up to 18 hours a day in their burrows and come out at night to hunt. When an armadillo leaves its burrow to eat, it moves around with its snout pressed to the ground. When the animal smells food, like insect **larvae**, it digs at the soil to uncover it. Then the animal sticks out its long tongue to slurp up the tasty treats. As an armadillo hunts, it stops to sniff the air, hoping to smell an ant nest or termite mound nearby.

When the armadillo has finished eating, it heads back to its burrow. The only traces the animal leaves behind are dozens of short, cone-shaped holes where it dug for food.

Fast Fact
Armadillos may travel far as they search for food.

▶ Armadillos have a very varied diet!

s

Armadillos use their long tongues to op ants out of their nests.

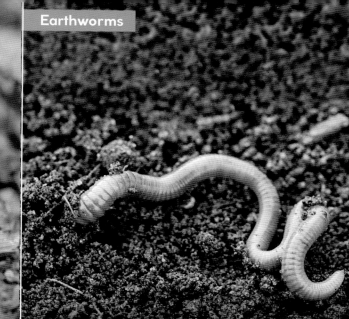

Earthworms

▶ Earthworms are easy to dig out of moist, loose soil.

vae

rmadillos claw at rotting wood to find ae such as mealworms and grubs.

Spiders

▶ Armadillos eat lots of invertebrates (animals without spines), like spiders.

Avoiding Trouble

Armadillos are sometimes **prey** for other animals. Predators may include alligators, pumas, jaguars, black bears, coyotes, and foxes.

When armadillos sense danger, they try to run to a burrow. They run in a zigzag pattern, making them hard to catch. Most species can run up to 30 miles (48.3 kilometers) per hour. But if there isn't time to run, they have other ways of protecting themselves.

The pichi can quickly dig a shallow hole and hide face-first. Its exposed shell-covered backside is hard for a predator to grab. Three-banded armadillos roll up into a ball. When threatened, a screaming hairy armadillo lets out a loud scream.

A nine-banded armadillo can jump several feet in the air, startling a predator and giving the armadillo time to run away. Or it can pull its head and feet into its shell and press its body to the ground. This makes the armadillo hard to flip over and keeps its soft belly out of reach.

◄ For this armadillo, jumping is a reflex—an automatic reaction.

In the Swim

You might be surprised to learn that armadillos are also at home in the water and can swim to escape danger. They may also hit the water to search for food or to look for a new place to live.

The armadillo has two ways of crossing a small stream or river. Because the animal is weighted down by its heavy shell, it sinks to the bottom. This enables it to walk across the bottom of a small river or stream. The armadillo can hold its breath while underwater—for up to six minutes!

An armadillo can also float across a waterway. First it swallows air to inflate its stomach and intestines. This makes it easy for the animal to float on the water's surface. Then the armadillo can swim, using its strong legs in a kind of dog paddle to get to the other side.

▶ An armadillo sinks underwater to walk across the bottom.

CHAPTER 3

Starting a Family

When an armadillo is one year old,
it is ready to start a family of its own. The **mating** season
varies. For some species, it can happen year-round. For
others, it takes place during the spring and summer.

When looking for a mate, a male nine-banded
armadillo approaches a female and sniffs her. If she isn't
interested, she may kick at the male until he leaves. If she
is interested, she wags her tail and the two pair up.

"Catch me if you can" describes the mating ritual of the
six-banded armadillo. A female runs wildly while several
males chase her. Eventually, one catches her and a match
is made.

Armadillos don't form lasting bonds. Once a pair of
armadillos has mated, the male and female don't stay
together. Females generally have only one mate per
season, but in some species males may mate with more
than one female.

▶ Male and female
pichis meet up only
to mate.

Pup Pup Hooray!

Two to five months after mating, a female armadillo is ready to give birth. She prepares a special birthing burrow, gathering soft grasses, straw, and leaves to make a nest. Then she hops backward into the nest to give birth.

Most armadillos have one or two babies, called pups, in a litter. But some species have many more. A nine-banded armadillo has four identical pups in each litter—all girls or all boys. Her pups weigh 1 to 4 oz. (28.3 to 113.4 g) at birth. She will have more than 50 pups in her lifetime. A seven-banded armadillo has eight to 15 pups in a single litter—and more than 100 offspring in a lifetime.

◀ Soft-skinned armadillo pups huddle for warmth.

In the Nursery

All newborn armadillo pups look like miniature adults without the hard shells. Their skin is gray, soft, and leathery. Within a few hours, they are able to walk. But they stay in the burrow while their skin hardens into a shell. This takes from a few days to a couple of weeks. Like all mammals, armadillos **nurse** their young.

Beyond that, however, there are some differences from species to species. Nine-banded pups are born with their eyes open. Southern three-banded armadillo pups can't see or hear for the first three weeks. All three-banded armadillo pups can roll into a ball when they're born.

The six-banded armadillo mother is very protective. If she senses danger, she moves her pups to a new burrow. The giant armadillo, more than any other species, is a dedicated parent. She has just one pup at a time and raises it for more than a year.

▶ **These nine-banded identical quadruplets are nursing together.**

28

Growing Strong

Pups stay close to their mothers for the first few weeks of life. After their shells have hardened, they accompany their mother on trips outside the burrow. They learn from their mother how to find food and what to eat. When they're about two months old, pups begin to eat insects while continuing to nurse. By four or five months, they stop nursing and **forage** for all their own food.

At nine to 12 months, pups are ready to head out on their own. Each pup will look for its own place to live and build its own burrows. Soon the offspring will be ready to start their own families. Most species move to areas away from their mothers. Not the giant armadillo, though. Even when it is old enough to go off on its own, the young giant armadillo continues to share its mother's burrow or uses one nearby. This is quite different from other species.

Armadillo lifespans vary by species, from four to more than 20 years in the wild. A pichi armadillo lives for about nine years, and a hairy armadillo can survive for 23 years or more.

◀ A three-banded armadillo mother stays close to her pup.

CHAPTER 4

Massive Ancestors

Huge mammals called glyptodonts

were the armadillo's ancient **ancestors**. These massive
animals, which lived millions of years ago, weighed about
4,400 lb. (1,995.8 kg). Glyptodonts were the size of a car
and had a built-in self-defense system. In addition to a
tough shell covered with bony plates that were 2 in.
(5.1 cm) thick, the glyptodont had a club-like tail. In some
species, the tail had a round knob at the end that was
covered in spikes.

Glyptodonts died out during the last Ice Age, about
11,000 years ago. Scientists aren't sure why they became
extinct. Some think that it was because of a rapidly
changing climate. Others think glyptodonts were
wiped out by humans who hunted them for their
shells, which were large enough to use for shelter.

▶ This glyptodont
weighed as much
as two horses!

Close Relatives

Anteaters, tree sloths, and armadillos are all related, though anteaters and trees sloths belong to one family and armadillos belong to another.

All three animals have a specialized backbone. That is what makes them close relatives. This extra-strong backbone makes armadillos and anteaters powerful diggers. They use their claws to dig for food. Sloths use these same features to climb and hang from trees.

Anteaters have long snouts and, like armadillos, they mostly eat insects. They use their sharp claws to tear into termite mounds and ant nests. Unlike armadillos, they lack teeth. Sloths do have small teeth, as armadillos do, and they also have slow metabolisms.

Aardvarks and pangolins share some physical characteristics with armadillos: long, sticky tongues, strong front legs, and claws for digging. However, these animals aren't related to armadillos.

◄ The three-toed sloth is the slowest mammal on Earth.

CHAPTER 5

Armadillos and Humans

Armadillos and humans have a long and complicated history. Armadillos cause problems for farmers, ranchers, and homeowners. When armadillos dig and loosen soil, it can be washed away by rain. And armadillo holes can trip and injure cattle and horses. Burrows dug under a porch or shed may damage a building or ruin a garden.

But armadillos can be helpful, too, by controlling pests. One armadillo can slurp up 40,000 ants in a single meal. And the nine-banded armadillo is the only animal in North America that eats fire ants. Fire ant bites are painful and can even be deadly to some people. This helpfulness might not be enough to keep armadillos safe from people, though.

▶ **This armadillo is crossing Route 66 in Arizona. Traffic can be deadly to armadillos.**

An Uncertain Future

Several armadillo species in South America are currently at risk. As more land gets developed for ranching and farming, species like the pichi, three-banded, long-nosed, and giant armadillos lose their habitat. Some people also hunt armadillos for their meat.

The giant armadillo is considered **vulnerable** to possible extinction. The Pantanal Giant Armadillo Project in southwestern Brazil was begun in 2011 to study these animals. Researchers use remotely operated cameras and radio tracking to observe the animals without disturbing them. So far, researchers have learned about giant armadillos' burrowing and mating habits, as well as their parenting skills.

The research has expanded to include several other armadillo species. With more knowledge, more can be done to help these animals survive and thrive.

▶ Researchers check the health of a giant armadillo.

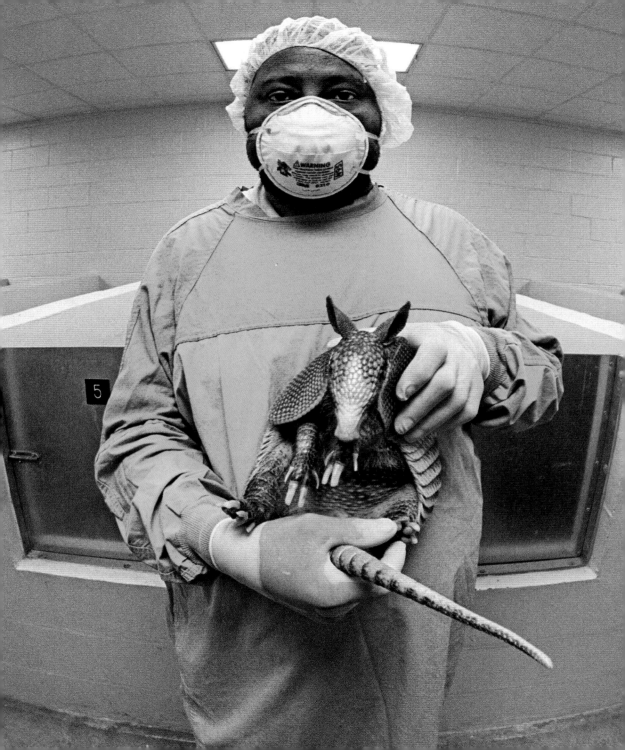

Nine-Banded Success

Nine-banded armadillos arrived in the United States more than 150 years ago. Scientists say they swam across the Rio Grande River from Mexico to southern Texas! So it's not surprising that these tough little animals are popular in Texas. In fact, elementary school students there fought to have the armadillo named the official state mammal. Other people wanted the longhorn cattle instead, but the students didn't give up. In the end, the longhorn was named the official large mammal, and the nine-banded armadillo became the official small mammal.

The nine-banded armadillos' fan base is growing even larger. Only they and humans can carry Hansen's disease (**leprosy**). Medical researchers use armadillos to learn about the disease. They are working to develop a **vaccine** to keep people from getting sick.

Armadillos may be small, but they contribute in a big way to the world around us.

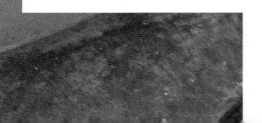

◄ A researcher holds a nine-banded armadillo.

Armadillo Family Tree

Armadillos are members of a group of animals that have a specialized backbone that helps them be powerful diggers. Their closest relatives are sloths and anteaters. Scientists are still trying to learn about these animals' common ancestor. This diagram shows how these animals are related. The closer together two animals are on the tree, the more alike they are.

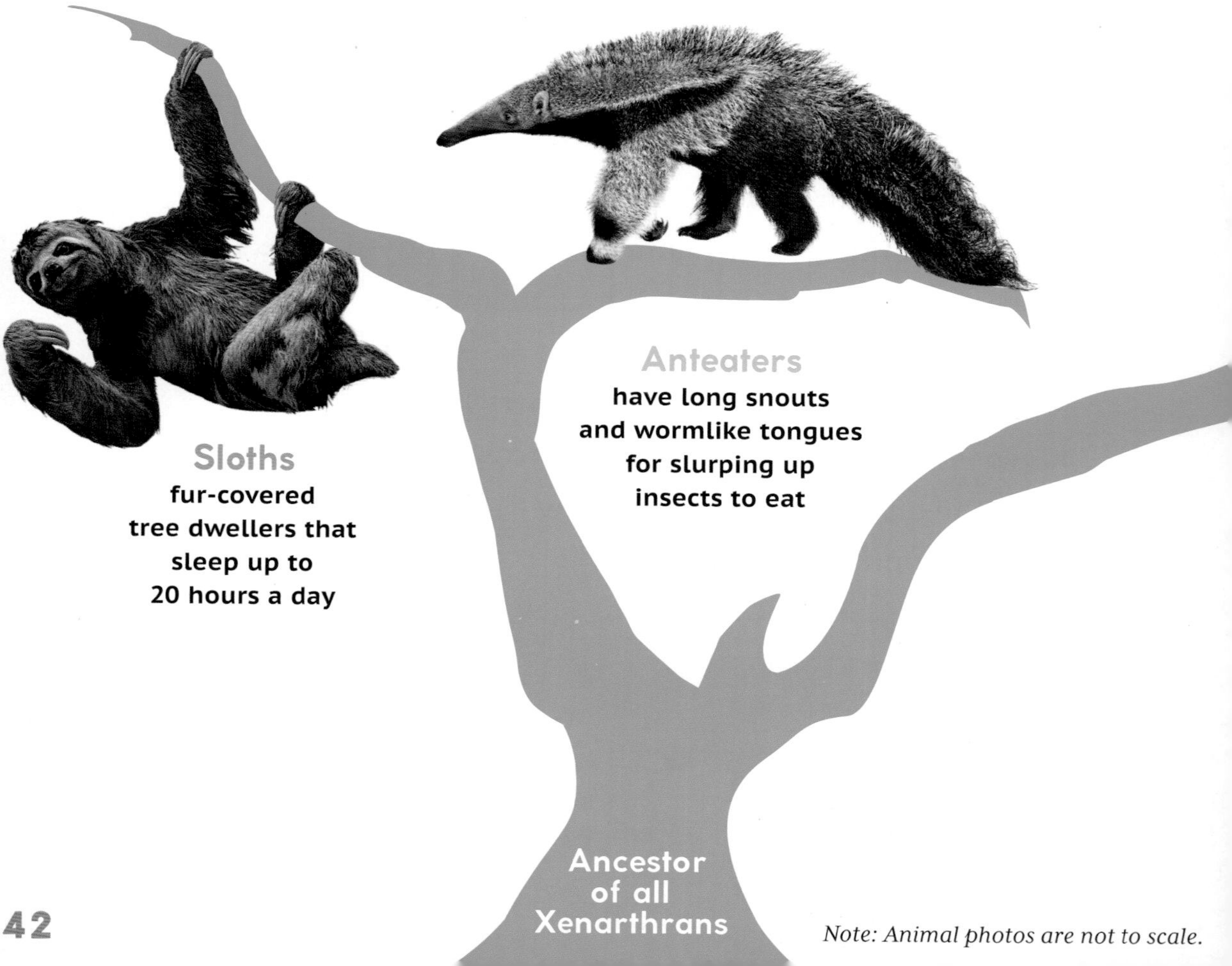

Anteaters
**have long snouts
and wormlike tongues
for slurping up
insects to eat**

Sloths
**fur-covered
tree dwellers that
sleep up to
20 hours a day**

**Ancestor
of all
Xenarthrans**

Note: Animal photos are not to scale.

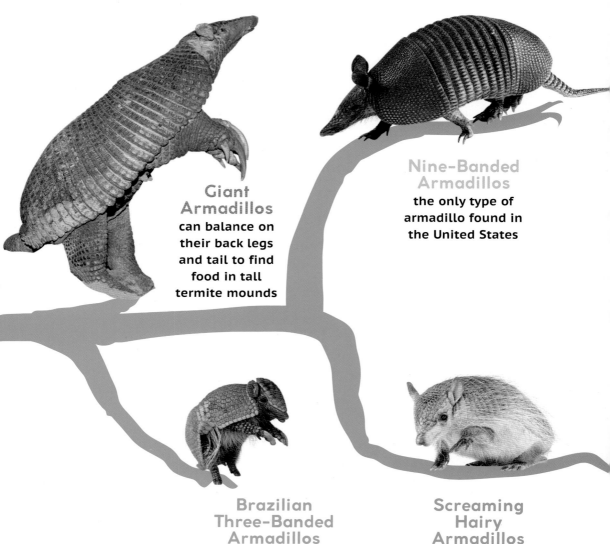

Giant Armadillos
can balance on their back legs and tail to find food in tall termite mounds

Nine-Banded Armadillos
the only type of armadillo found in the United States

Brazilian Three-Banded Armadillos
one of only two species that can roll into a ball for protection

Screaming Hairy Armadillos
have long hairs on their bodies and squeal when threatened

Words to Know

A .... **ancestors** (*ANN-ses-turs*) family members that lived long ago

B .... **burrows** (*BUR-ohs*) tunnels or holes in the ground made or used as homes by animals

C .... **carapace** (*KARE-uh-pis*) hard upper shell of an armadillo, turtle, arachnid, or crustacean

carrion (*KAHR-ee-on*) the flesh of dead animals

D .... **drought** (*DROUT*) a long period without rain

E .... **extinct** (*ik-STINGKT*) no longer found alive

F .... **forage** (*FOR-ij*) to go in search of food

G .... **glands** (*GLANDZ*) organs in the body that produce or release natural chemicals

H .... **habitats** (*HAB-i-tats*) the places where an animal or plant is usually found

K .... **keen** (*KEEN*) highly developed

L .... **larvae** (*LAHR-vee*) insects at the state of development between an egg and a pupa, when they look like worms

leprosy (*LEH-pruh-see*) a contagious disease affecting the skin and nerves

litter (*LIT-ur*) a group of animals born at the same time to one mother

M .... **mammals** (*MAM-uhlz*) warm-blooded animals that have hair or fur and usually give birth to live babies; female mammals produce milk to feed their young

mating (*MAY-ting*) joining together to produce babies

metabolism *(muh-TAB-uh-liz-uhm)* the process in our body that changes food we eat into energy we need to breathe, digest, and grow

N......... **nocturnal** *(nahk-TUR-nuhl)* active at night

nurse *(NURS)* to feed a baby milk from a breast

O......... **omnivores** *(AHM-nuh-vorz)* animals or people that eat both plants and meat

P......... **predator** *(PRED-uh-tuhr)* an animal that lives by hunting other animals for food

prey *(PRAY)* an animal that is hunted by another animal for food

S......... **savanna** *(suh-VAN-uh)* a flat, grassy plain with few or no trees

scutes *(SCOOTZ)* flexible pieces of fingernail-like material that form a shell

snouts *(SNOUTZ)* long front parts of animals' heads; a snout includes the nose, mouth, and jaws

species *(SPEE-sheez)* one of the groups into which animals and plants are divided; members of the same species can mate and have offspring

V......... **vaccine** *(vak-SEEN)* a substance containing dead, weakened, or living organisms that can be injected or taken orally to protect someone from a disease

vulnerable *(VUHL-nur-uh-buhl)* facing threats and likely to become endangered

Find Out More

BOOKS

- Llanas, Sheila Griffin. *Armadillos* (Animal Icons). Minneapolis, MN: Checkerboard Library, 2013.

- McKerley, Jennifer Guess. *Amazing Armadillos*. New York: Random House Children's Books, 2009.

- Phillips, Dee. *Armadillo's Burrow*. New York: Bearport Publishing, 2013.

- Potts, Steve. *Armadillos*. Mankato, MN: Capstone Press, 2012.

- Riggs, Kate. *Armadillos* (Amazing Animals). Mankato, MN: Creative Company, 2018.

To find more books and resources about animals, visit:
scholastic.com

Index

Index *(continued)*

About the Author

Susan Knopf is a writer and book editor. Her favorite topics are science, space, and animals. She has produced books for Animal Planet and Discovery, written about gross science, and edited books based on Reading Rainbow. Susan saw many armadillos while traveling in Texas and hopes to see one swimming sometime soon.